Cambridge English

Flyers 9

Answer Booklet

Cambridge University Press
www.cambridge.org/elt

Cambridge English Language Assessment
www.cambridgeenglish.org

Information on this title: www.cambridge.org/9781107464278

© Cambridge University Press and UCLES 2015

First published 2015
Reprinted 2015

Printed in Italy by Rotolito Lombarda S.p.A.

A catalogue record for this publication is available from the British Library

ISBN 978-1-107-46431-5 Student's Book
ISBN 978-1-107-46427-8 Answer Booklet
ISBN 978-1-107-46430-8 Audio CD

Contents

Introduction

The *Cambridge English: Young Learners* tests offer an elementary-level testing system (up to CEFR level A2) for learners of English between the ages of 7 and 12. The tests include three key levels of assessment: *Starters*, *Movers* and *Flyers*.

Flyers is the third level in the system. Test instructions are very simple and consist only of words and structures specified in the syllabus.

The complete test lasts about one hour and a quarter and has the following components: Listening, Reading and Writing, and Speaking.

	length	number of parts	number of questions
Listening	approx. 25 minutes	5	25
Reading and Writing	40 minutes	7	50
Speaking	approx. 7–9 minutes	4	–

Candidates need a pen or pencil for the Reading and Writing paper, and coloured pens or pencils for the Listening paper. All answers are written on the question papers.

Listening

In general, the aim is to focus on the 'here and now' and to use language in meaningful contexts. In addition to multiple-choice and short-answer questions, candidates are asked to use coloured pencils to mark their responses to one task. There are five parts. Each part begins with a clear example.

part	main skill focus	input	expected response	number of questions
1	the main skill focus in all five parts of the Listening test is listening for specific information of various kinds, e.g. numbers, describing people etc.	picture, names and dialogue	draw lines to match names to people in a picture	5
2		form or page of notepad with missing words and dialogue	write words or numbers in gaps	5
3		picture sets and list of illustrated words or names and dialogue	match pictures with illustrated word or name by writing letter in box	5
4		3-option multiple-choice pictures and dialogues	tick box under correct picture	5
5		picture and dialogue	carry out instructions to colour, draw and write (range of colours is: black, blue, brown, green, grey, orange, pink, purple, red, yellow)	5

Reading and Writing

Again, the focus is on the 'here and now' and the use of language in meaningful contexts where possible. To complete the test, candidates need a single pen or pencil of any colour. There are seven parts, each starting with a clear example.

part	main skill focus	input	expected response	number of questions
1	reading definitions and matching to words copying words	nouns and definitions	copy the correct words next to the definitions	10
2	reading sentences about a picture and writing one-word answers	picture and sentences	write 'yes' or 'no'	7
3	reading and completing a continuous dialogue	half a dialogue with responses in a box	select correct response and write A–H in gap	5
4	reading for specific information and gist copying words	gapped text with words in a box	choose and copy missing words correctly tick a box to choose the best title for the story	6
5	reading and understanding a story completing sentences	story, picture and gapped sentences	complete sentences about story by writing 1, 2, 3 or 4 words	7
6	reading story copying words	gapped text and 3-option multiple choice (grammatical words)	complete text by selecting the correct words and copying them in corresponding gaps	10
7	reading and understanding a short text (e.g. page from diary or letter) providing words	gapped text	write words in gaps no answer options given	5

Speaking

In the Speaking test, the candidate speaks with one examiner for about eight minutes. The format of the test is explained in advance to the child in their native language, by a teacher or person familiar to them. This person then takes the child into the exam room and introduces them to the examiner.

Speaking ability is assessed according to various criteria, including comprehension, the ability to produce a prompt, appropriate and accurate response, and pronunciation.

part	main skill focus	input	expected response
1	understanding statements and responding with differences	two (one is the examiner's) similar pictures oral statements about examiner's picture	identify six differences in candidate's picture from oral statements about examiner's picture
2	responding to questions with short answers and forming questions to elicit information	one set of facts and one set of question cues	answer and ask questions about two people, objects or situations
3	understanding the beginning of a story and then continuing it based on a series of pictures	picture sequence	describe each picture in turn
4	understanding and responding to personal questions	open-ended questions about candidate	answer personal questions

Further information

Further information about *Cambridge English: Young Learners* can be obtained from:

Cambridge English Language Assessment
1 Hills Road
Cambridge CB1 2EU
United Kingdom

www.cambridgeenglish.org/help
www.cambridgeenglish.org/younglearners

Test 1 Answers

Listening

Part 1 (5 marks)

Lines should be drawn between:

1 Emma and the girl standing by a rock, waving
2 Richard and the boy having his photo taken, holding an ice cream
3 Betty and the girl playing with sand, with a flag
4 William and the boy holding a duck, wearing spotted shorts
5 Katy and the girl in a blue sweater, holding a camera

Part 2 (5 marks)

1 Boyles (correct spelling) 2 flowers 3 35/thirty-five
4 insects 5 bus

Part 3 (5 marks)

1 glue – E – under newspaper 2 ring – H – cooker
3 diary – G – by bed 4 watch – C – coat pocket
5 phone – F – outside

Part 4 (5 marks)

1 C 2 B 3 C 4 B 5 A

Part 5 (5 marks)

1 Colour the suitcase in the man's hand – red
2 Draw and colour a star on the computer – blue
3 Write 'DAY' on the clock after 'HAVE A GOOD'
4 Colour the magazine on the wall – pink
5 Colour the rucksack on the boy's back – brown

TRANSCRIPT *Hello. This is the Cambridge English Flyers Listening Test.*

Part 1 *Listen and look. There is one example.*

[pause]

GIRL: I had lots of fun with my friends on Sunday, Uncle Robert. Look at this photo!
MAN: Wow, what a nice beach! It looks very sunny there.
GIRL: It was. Can you see Jim? The boy with blond hair in the water?
MAN: Yes.
GIRL: He swam all the way to that island!

[pause]

Can you see the line? This is an example. Now you listen and draw lines.

[pause]

1
MAN: Who's that girl?
GIRL: The girl who's waving by the rocks?
MAN: Yes.
GIRL: Oh, that's Emma. We saw lots of little fish in the water there.

[pause]

2
MAN: And what about that boy there? Who's he?
GIRL: In the sailing boat?
MAN: No, the one with the ice cream. He's standing next to the girl in the purple T-shirt.
GIRL: Oh, you mean Richard. He's in my class. I like him a lot.

[pause]

3
GIRL: And there's Betty. She's my very best friend.

MAN:	The girl with the comic?
GIRL:	No, I mean the girl who's playing. She's just put that little flag in the sand.
MAN:	Oh, yes.

[pause]

4

MAN:	Did you go swimming that day?
GIRL:	No. The water was too cold for me. But William did. Can you see him?
MAN:	Is that the boy with the duck?
GIRL:	Yes, in spotted shorts. He's not in the water here, but he went swimming later.
MAN:	Oh.

[pause]

5

GIRL:	Katy's smiling here, but she didn't have a very good day.
MAN:	Which one's she?
GIRL:	There … in the blue sweater … with the camera, but she lost it in the afternoon. She went in the sea with it and dropped it.
MAN:	Oh dear!
GIRL:	Mmm … but her dad's going to buy her a new one.
MAN:	Well, that's good …

[pause]

Now listen to Part 1 again.

[pause]

[The recording is repeated.]

That is the end of Part 1.

[pause]

Part 2   *Listen and look. There is one example.*

[pause]

BOY:	What are we going to do in our lesson today, Miss Gold?
WOMAN:	We're going to talk about the class visit to Sunny Farm, David.
BOY:	Great! When are we going to go?
WOMAN:	Next Monday. Write it down, then you won't forget.
BOY:	OK.

[pause]

Can you see the answer? Now you listen and write.

[pause]

WOMAN:	We're going to meet the farmer there.
BOY:	What's his name? Do you know?
WOMAN:	Yes. It's Mr Boyles. That's B-O-Y-L-E-S.
BOY:	OK. I've written that down too. What does he grow there? Vegetables?
WOMAN:	No. He grows flowers and then he sells them to people in other countries.

BOY:	Wow. I've never seen that kind of farm before. Is it a big farm, Miss Gold, with lots of fields?
WOMAN:	Well, David, he has thirty-five fields. It's a very interesting farm to visit.
BOY:	Great. But what will we do there?
WOMAN:	I'd like you to do some drawing there. We'll learn about his work first and then he's going to show you his insects. They're his hobby. I want you all to draw them.
BOY:	Oh! I don't like them. Do we have to do that?
WOMAN:	Yes. They aren't dangerous ones, David! The farmer keeps them in big boxes in his house. You don't have to pick them up if you don't want to.
BOY:	Good! And are we going to go to the farm by car?
WOMAN:	We thought about that, but then we decided not to. We're going to go in the school bus.
BOY:	That sounds exciting!
WOMAN:	Yes, it'll be a good day, I'm sure.

[pause]

Now listen to Part 2 again.

[pause]

[The recording is repeated.]

That is the end of Part 2.

[pause]

Part 3   *Listen and look. There is one example.*

[pause]

Harry is very good at finding things for other people. Where did he find each thing?

[pause]

WOMAN:	Oh, Harry, I need to drive to town but …
MAN:	… But, I know, you can't find your car keys.
WOMAN:	That's right!
MAN:	I found them on the sofa. I'll go and get them for you.

[pause]

Can you see the letter B? Now you listen and write a letter in each box.

[pause]

WOMAN:	You're very clever at finding things, Harry.
MAN:	Thank you! Someone at work couldn't find the glue yesterday. He got very angry about it, but I found it after a few minutes. It was under a newspaper on his desk! He was very happy when I gave it to him.

[pause]

MAN: I like finding things for people.

WOMAN: Well, you helped my mother last week, didn't you?

MAN: Oh yes, when she lost her ring ... that was more difficult to find. It was in her kitchen – next to the cooker. She burnt her hand when she was cooking some lunch for me and she had to take it off. Oh ... is she OK now?

WOMAN: Oh, yes. She's fine.

[pause]

MAN: And Ben asked me to help him find his diary yesterday. We looked everywhere for it. In his cupboard ... in his sports bag ...

WOMAN: Did you find it?

MAN: Yes. There were two or three other books on top of it on the floor by his bed.

WOMAN: Hmmm.

[pause]

WOMAN: But you lose things too sometimes ...

MAN: Of course I do. I couldn't find my gold watch on Sunday. I took it off in the bathroom but it wasn't there when I went to look for it. So I looked in the pockets of my coat next and I found it there.

[pause]

MAN: Oh ... and take this with you when you go to town. You might need it.

WOMAN: What is it?

MAN: Your phone! You used it this morning when we had breakfast outside. I brought it back inside for you.

WOMAN: Oh, thanks.

[pause]

Now listen to Part 3 again.

[The recording is repeated.]

That is the end of Part 3.

[pause]

Part 4 *Listen and look. There is one example.*

[pause]

Where's Michael?

[pause]

WOMAN: Michael! Where are you? Are you outside?

BOY: No, Mum, I'm down here in the basement. What do you want?

WOMAN: Can you come upstairs for a minute? I'm in the living room. I want to talk to you.

BOY: OK.

[pause]

Can you see the tick? Now you listen and tick the box.

[pause]

1 What must Michael paint first?

WOMAN: Good ... Now, you're going to help me today, aren't you?

BOY: Yes. We're going to paint the wall in the garden, aren't we?

WOMAN: Yes, but can you paint the garden chairs first? They're more important.

BOY: OK. And I want to paint my bike later too.

[pause]

2 What must Michael wear?

WOMAN: Take that sweater off, Michael. You'll get paint on it.

BOY: But it's old ...

WOMAN: I know, but it's nice too. And take your jeans off and put your old shorts on. It's nice and warm outside.

BOY: My grey ones?

WOMAN: Yes.

[pause]

3 What can Michael eat?

WOMAN: Would you like a snack first?

BOY: Yes, please. Can I have some chocolate biscuits?

WOMAN: Mmm. Not that kind of snack ... how about some soup? I made some this morning.

BOY: All right. And can I have some more of that lovely bread with it?

WOMAN: Sorry, Michael. Dad had the last piece for breakfast.

BOY: Oh!

[pause]

4 Where's the paint that Michael needs?

BOY: Where's the paint, Mum? Behind the kitchen door?

WOMAN: No, that's not the right kind. You need the paint that's in the cupboard.

BOY: Under the stairs?

WOMAN: Yes. And the brushes are on the kitchen shelf in a big plastic bag.

BOY: OK. I'll go and fetch them too.

[pause]

5 What's the matter with Michael now?

BOY: Oh ... ouch!

WOMAN: What's the matter now?

BOY: I've just dropped the paint. It fell on my foot. Ow, it hurts!

WOMAN: Come here. Let me see ... You're OK.

BOY: Yesterday I hurt my arm when I fell out of the tree, and last week I hit my nose on the glass door! Can't I just stay inside and play games?

WOMAN: No!

[pause]

Now listen to Part 4 again.

[The recording is repeated.]

That is the end of Part 4.

[pause]

Part 5   *Listen and look at the picture. There is one example.*

[pause]

GIRL: Are the people in this picture inside a restaurant or a hotel?
MAN: They're in a hotel. They're going to stay there.
GIRL: Oh ... Shall I colour something here? Can I colour the lamp on the little table?
MAN: Yes, please. Make it yellow.
GIRL: OK.

[pause]

Can you see the yellow lamp? This is an example.

Now you listen and colour and draw and write.

[pause]

1

GIRL: What else can I colour?
MAN: Ermm ... how about the suitcase – the one that the man's carrying?
GIRL: OK. It looks heavy! Which colour shall I use?
MAN: I think red is a good colour for that.
GIRL: All right.

[pause]

2

GIRL: Can I draw something in the picture now?
MAN: Yes. Draw a star on the computer.
GIRL: All right. I'll draw a nice, big one.
MAN: Good, now colour it blue.
GIRL: OK. I'll do that now.

[pause]

3

GIRL: And can I write something too?
MAN: Yes. OK. Look at the clock. It's got words on it, but one word is missing. 'Have a good ...' Can you see that?
GIRL: Yes. What's the missing word?
MAN: Day! Write that there for me, please.
GIRL: That's easy!

[pause]

4

MAN: Now some more colouring ... Colour the magazine, please.
GIRL: The one in front of the woman?

MAN: Not that one. There's another one ... look ... up there under all the postcards. Colour that one pink.
GIRL: All right.

[pause]

5

GIRL: Can I colour the umbrella now?
MAN: No, we don't need to colour that. Colour the rucksack on the boy's back, please.
GIRL: OK. Shall I use my brown pencil for that?
MAN: Yes.
GIRL: Right. It's finished, I think.
MAN: Great!

[pause]

Now listen to Part 5 again.

[The recording is repeated.]

That is the end of the Flyers Listening Test.

Reading and Writing

Part 1 (10 marks)

1 gloves   2 an airport   3 a fridge
4 a dinosaur   5 a knife   6 a swan   7 tights
8 a museum   9 scarves   10 a factory

Part 2 (7 marks)

1 no   2 yes   3 no   4 yes   5 no   6 no
7 yes

Part 3 (5 marks)

1 G   2 B   3 C   4 H   5 A

Part 4 (6 marks)

1 presents   2 look   3 woke   4 ready
5 blanket   6 Emma's busy day

Part 5 (7 marks)

1 supermarket   2 (Jack's) mum
3 an ambulance   4 a/the doctor
5 (some) sweets   6 phoned
7 go (back) to (his/the) school

Part 6 (10 marks)

1 to   2 brought   3 didn't   4 each
5 buy   6 on   7 so   8 There   9 too
10 have

Part 7 (5 marks)

1 in/at   2 team(s)   3 than   4 do
5 about

Speaking

Part	Examiner does this:	Examiner says this:	Minimum response expected from child:	Back-up questions:
	Usher brings candidate in.	Usher to Examiner: **Hello, this is** (**child's name***).		
		Examiner: **Hello, *. My name's** *Jane/Ms Smith*.	**Hello.**	
		What's your surname?	*Silver*	**What's your family name?**
		How old are you?	*ten*	**Are you *ten*?**
1	Shows candidate both **Find the Differences** pictures. Points to the mountains in each picture.	**Now, here are two pictures. My picture is nearly the same as yours, but some things are different.** **For example, in my picture there are two mountains, but in your picture there are three. OK?**		
	Describes things without pointing.	**I'm going to say something about my picture. You tell me how your picture is different.**		1. Point at relevant difference/s. 2. Repeat statement. 3. Ask back-up question.
		In my picture, there's a scarf on the ground. It's green and pink.	*In my picture, the scarf's purple and yellow.*	**What colour is the scarf?**
		In my picture, there are some clouds in the sky.	*In my picture, there aren't any clouds.*	**Are there any clouds?**
		In my picture, the people with the sledge are on the left.	*In my picture, they're on the right.*	**Where are the people with the sledge?**
		In my picture, the tables are round.	*In my picture, they're square.*	**Are the tables round?**
		In my picture, the boy's putting some gloves on the snowman.	*In my picture, the boy's putting a hat on the snowman.*	**What's the boy putting on the snowman?**
		In my picture, the black dog is bigger than the brown dog.	*In my picture, the brown dog is bigger.*	**Which dog is bigger?**
2	Shows candidate both **CD** information pages. Then points to candidate's information page.	**Mary and Tony like listening to music. I don't know anything about Mary's favourite song, but you do. So I'm going to ask you some questions.**		
	Points to the girl on candidate's information page. Asks the questions.	**What's the name of the singer?** **How often does she listen to the song?** **Where does she listen to it?** **Is the music fast or slow?** **Do her friends like the song?**	*Ben Star* *every day* *(in her) bedroom* *(it's) slow* *Yes, (they like it) a lot.*	Point at the information if necessary.
	Points to the boy on candidate's information page.	**Now you don't know anything about Tony's favourite song, so you ask me some questions.**		

*Remember to use the child's name throughout the test.

Part	Examiner does this:	Examiner says this:	Minimum response expected from child:	Back-up questions:
	Responds using information on examiner's information page.	In the car. It's fast. Every weekend. No, not much. Alex Moon	*Where does Tony listen to the song?* *Is the music fast or slow?* *How often does he listen to the song?* *Do his friends like the song?* *What's the name of the singer?*	Point at information cues if necessary.
3	Shows candidate **Picture Story**. Allows time to look at the pictures.	These pictures tell a story. It's called 'Pat and Robert lose a picture'. Just look at the pictures first. Pat's cutting out pictures of animals. Robert's gluing them into a book. Grandma's bringing them some juice. Now you tell the story.		1. Point at the pictures. 2. Ask questions about the pictures.
			Robert's putting a picture of an elephant on the sofa.	**What's Robert doing?**
			Grandma's sitting on the sofa. They're all drinking the juice.	**Where's Grandma sitting?**
			Grandma's sleeping.	**What's Grandma doing now?**
			The children are looking for the picture of the elephant.	What are the children doing now?
			Grandma's going now. She's got the picture on her back!	**What's Grandma got on her back?**
			The children are laughing.	What are the children doing?
4	Puts the pictures away and turns to the candidate.	Now, let's talk about what you do after school. What time do your lessons finish?	*(at) 3 o'clock*	Do your lessons finish at *3 o'clock*?
		How do you go home?	*(by) bike*	Do you go home by *bike*?
		Where do you do your homework?	*(in my) bedroom*	Do you do your homework *in your bedroom*?
		What do you have for dinner?	*chicken*	Do you have *chicken* for dinner?
		Tell me about the things that you do in the evening.	*play computer games*	Do you *play computer games*?
			phone my friends	Do you *phone your friends*?
			watch television	Do you *watch television*?
		OK, thank you, *. Goodbye.	Goodbye.	

*Remember to use the child's name throughout the test.

Test 2 Answers

Listening

Part 1 (5 marks)

Lines should be drawn between:

1 Emma and the girl who's whispering, brushing her hair
2 Harry and the boy skating
3 Vicky and the woman by the swans, reading a newspaper
4 Michael and the boy in the black jacket, skipping
5 Katy and the girl in yellow shorts, playing with the dog

Part 2 (5 marks)

1 Welcome (correct spelling)   2 4/four   3 white
4 bikes/bicycles   5 12th/12

Part 3 (5 marks)

1 Betty – H – photos of houses
2 William – A – telephone
3 Mary – C – meeting room
4 Peter – F – letters
5 Jane – G – tea and biscuits

Part 4 (5 marks)

1 C   2 A   3 B   4 B   5 C

Part 5 (5 marks)

1 Colour the umbrella in the corner – orange
2 Colour the toy castle on the floor – brown
3 Draw and colour a bird in the sky outside – green
4 Write 'PAINT' on the box
5 Colour the diary by the light – red

TRANSCRIPT   *Hello. This is the Cambridge English Flyers Listening Test.*

Part 1   *Listen and look. There is one example.*

[pause]

GIRL: We went to the park today, Grandpa. We had a nice time there. Look!
MAN: Oh, yes. Who's that? The person who's lying on the grass.
GIRL: That's Richard. He's one of Dad's friends.
MAN: Why is his hat on his face like that?
GIRL: Because it was very sunny.

[pause]

Can you see the line? This is an example.

Now you listen and draw lines.

[pause]

1

MAN: Who's that girl? The one who's whispering to her friend?
GIRL: The one who's brushing her hair? Oh, that's Emma. She's got a secret!
MAN: What is it?
GIRL: I can't tell you, Grandpa! She's one of my best friends!

[pause]

2

GIRL: There's Harry. He came with us too. He lives in the house that's next to ours.
MAN: Is that the boy on the swing?
GIRL: No, the one with the skates on. He can go so fast on his skates!
MAN: Does he ever fall over?
GIRL: Sometimes.

[pause]

3

GIRL: Mum's friend, Vicky, came too. She's there by the swans.
MAN: The woman who's reading a newspaper?
GIRL: Yes. It was about the queen and her family.
MAN: Oh!
GIRL: She said it was interesting …

[pause]

4

MAN: And who's the boy in the black jacket?
GIRL: You mean Michael! The boy who's skipping?
MAN: Yes. Why's he doing that?
GIRL: Because your legs get stronger if you do that.
MAN: I must remember that!

[pause]

5

GIRL: And another friend of mine, Katy, was there when we arrived.
MAN: The girl in the yellow dress?
GIRL: No, that's her sister. My friend's got yellow shorts on.
MAN: And is that her dog? The one she's playing with?
GIRL: Yes. We had lots of fun with him that afternoon.

[pause]

Now listen to Part 1 again.

[The recording is repeated.]

That is the end of Part 1.

[pause]

Part 2 Listen and look. There is one example.

[pause]

WOMAN: Hello! Are you the farmer's son?
BOY: Yes, I am. Can I help you?
WOMAN: Our book says we can camp on this farm. Is that right?
BOY: Yes, it is. Dad's not here this morning, but I can help. How many nights do you want to stay here?
WOMAN: Five.
BOY: OK!

[pause]

Can you see the answer? Now you listen and write.

[pause]

BOY: And what's your name, please?
WOMAN: We're Mr and Mrs Welcome. You spell that W-E-L-C-O-M-E.
BOY: OK … I'll just write that on this piece of paper.
WOMAN: We've got our children too. There are four of us.

BOY: That's fine. Perhaps your children would like to come and see the sheep one day with me! I help my dad a lot here.
WOMAN: I can see that!
BOY: What colour is your tent?
WOMAN: It's blue with a white stripe round it. It's not very big.
BOY: OK … You can put it in our top field. You can drive up there.
WOMAN: Great. We've got lots of camping things to carry, so that's good!
BOY: Do you need anything?
WOMAN: We've got cooking and sleeping things but have you got any bikes we can use? We might want to go for a ride.
BOY: Yes. We can help with those. Dad will come and speak to you about that.
WOMAN: Thanks a lot. The countryside here is so beautiful!
BOY: And when are you going to leave?
WOMAN: On June 11th, sorry … I mean June 12th. My mistake!
BOY: That's all right. OK … Follow me and I'll show you where to put your tent now.
WOMAN: Great! Thanks!

[pause]

Now listen to Part 2 again.

[The recording is repeated.]

That is the end of Part 2.

[pause]

Part 3 Listen and look. There is one example.

[pause]

Mrs Dance is telling her daughter, Sarah, about the people in her office and about their different jobs. What job does each person do?

[pause]

GIRL: Hello, Mum. You look tired.
WOMAN: Well, we all had a busy day in our office today, Sarah. Lots of people came in with questions about buying and selling houses, and David had to read and write hundreds of answers to emails on his computer. He never stops working!

[pause]

Can you see the letter E? Now you listen and write a letter in each box.

[pause]

GIRL: Who else works at your office now?
WOMAN: Well, a woman who's called Betty has just started. She's working hard too. She has to take the photos of houses or flats that we're selling for people. It's a nice job, I think.
GIRL: Yes, it sounds fun!

[pause]

WOMAN: And William's always busy too. He spends a lot of time on the telephone. He's very good at talking to people. If people get angry, he can make them happy again! He's very friendly.

GIRL: And clever too?

WOMAN: Yes, that's right!

[pause]

GIRL: And did you have any important meetings this afternoon, Mum?

WOMAN: Yes, Sarah. Mary made the meeting room look very nice. That's her job. She gets all the chairs ready. But she's got lots of other jobs too, of course. She doesn't only do that.

[pause]

WOMAN: A student from the college started work today too. He wants to learn all about business.

GIRL: What's his name?

WOMAN: He's called Peter. We asked him to go to the post office to buy stamps and post all the letters. There were lots to carry and it's a long walk there, so he was tired. He hasn't learnt to drive yet.

[pause]

WOMAN: But the most important person in the office is Jane.

GIRL: Why? What's her job?

WOMAN: She brings us our tea and biscuits! She's lovely. She comes and talks to everyone too. She's very kind. But she doesn't clean the office. Someone else comes and does that in the evenings when we aren't there.

GIRL: That's good.

[pause]

Now listen to Part 3 again.

[The recording is repeated.]

That is the end of Part 3.

[pause]

Part 4 *Listen and look. There is one example.*

[pause]

What time must Robert get up in the morning?

[pause]

BOY: I'm going to go to bed now, Mum. It's eight o'clock.

WOMAN: But it's so early, Robert.

BOY: Yes, but I have to get up at half past five. I've got to leave at quarter past six in the morning, remember! Our class is going to go to London tomorrow.

WOMAN: All right.

[pause]

Can you see the tick? Now you listen and tick the box.

[pause]

1 What's Robert going to wear tomorrow?

WOMAN: Get your clothes ready tonight, Robert. Do you have to wear your school uniform?

BOY: Not this time. We can go in jeans.

WOMAN: OK. And will you wear your new sweater?

BOY: No, just a shirt, Mum.

[pause]

2 What will Robert go and see in London first?

WOMAN: So ... you're going to visit the science museum?

BOY: Yes, in the afternoon. But first we're going to walk across the most famous bridge in London!

WOMAN: That'll be exciting. You're going to have a picnic next to the lake too, aren't you?

BOY: Yes, that'll be in the afternoon too.

[pause]

3 How will Robert and his friends go to London?

WOMAN: I'll take you to the station in the car. OK?

BOY: Thanks, Mum. My friends and I are going to enjoy going on the train to London.

WOMAN: Buses are fun too!

BOY: Yes, but only if you can sit at the front.

[pause]

4 What will Robert buy in London?

WOMAN: I'll give you some money. You might want to buy something in London.

BOY: Thanks. But I'll only get postcards. Nothing else.

WOMAN: Not a T-shirt or a flag? They sell lots of those in the shops in London.

BOY: I know, but I don't need those.

[pause]

5 Where does Robert want to go one day in London?

BOY: Can we go to London one day? You, me and Dad?

WOMAN: Of course! I'd like to go to the theatre there. And Dad wants to go to the space museum. What about you?

BOY: I'd like to visit one of the football clubs and see the players there.

WOMAN: Mm, Dad too, I think!

[pause]

Now listen to Part 4 again.

[The recording is repeated.]

That is the end of Part 4.

[pause]

Part 5 *Listen and look at the picture. There is one example.*

[pause]

BOY: This artist's picture looks good, but what is he drawing? Is it an octopus?
WOMAN: Yes. He draws lots of pictures of animals and different kinds of fish.
BOY: Well, can I colour it? Can I make it pink?
WOMAN: All right! Do that now!
BOY: OK!

[pause]

Can you see the pink octopus? This is an example.

Now you listen and colour and draw and write.

[pause]

1

BOY: What shall I colour next?
WOMAN: How about the umbrella? The one in the corner.
BOY: OK. Which pencil shall I use to colour it?
WOMAN: Have you got an orange one? Use that!
BOY: All right!

[pause]

2

WOMAN: Now ... can you see the castle?
BOY: Do you mean the one in the picture on the wall?
WOMAN: No, I mean the toy one on the floor. Colour that brown now, please.
BOY: OK. I'm doing that now. Who plays with it?
WOMAN: I don't know.

[pause]

3

BOY: I'd like to draw something too. Can I do that?
WOMAN: Yes, that's a good idea. What would you like to draw?
BOY: Well, the window's open. Can I draw a bird outside in the sky?
WOMAN: Yes, you can. And colour it green.
BOY: All right!

[pause]

4

WOMAN: I'd like you to write something here too, please. Can you see the box on the bottom shelf?
BOY: Yes. Must I write on that?
WOMAN: Yes, please. Write 'PAINT' on that. He puts all his things in it at the end of each day.
BOY: So he's a tidy artist!
WOMAN: Yes, he is!

[pause]

5

WOMAN: And perhaps you should colour the artist's diary now.
BOY: The one by the light?
WOMAN: That's right. Colour it purple.
BOY: Can I colour it red, because I've got that pencil in my hand?
WOMAN: Of course you can. That's fine. And well done! We've finished now.
BOY: Great! Thank you!

[pause]

Now listen to Part 5 again.

[The recording is repeated.]

That is the end of the Flyers Listening Test.

Reading and Writing

Part 1 (10 marks)

1 an airport   2 a clown   3 a university
4 a hospital   5 a giraffe   6 a dentist
7 a spider   8 a factory   9 a dolphin
10 a policeman

Part 2 (7 marks)

1 no   2 no   3 no   4 yes   5 no   6 no
7 yes

Part 3 (5 marks)

1 F   2 D   3 A   4 H   5 G

Part 4 (6 marks)

1 thirsty   2 snows   3 walked   4 torch
5 walls   6 My day at the pyramids

Part 5 (7 marks)

1 (new) (school) books
2 afraid/scared/nervous of/about (starting/beginning/going to)
3 came/was/arrived early   4 started/drove off (suddenly)
5 picked up   6 Mrs Green   7 (snack) shop

Part 6 (10 marks)

1 also   2 than   3 if   4 want   5 of
6 Some   7 until   8 them   9 over
10 where

Part 7 (5 marks)

1 on (my)   2 took/got   3 ate/had/enjoyed // eat/have/enjoy   4 at/on/near   5 have/'ve

Speaking

Part	Examiner does this:	Examiner says this:	Minimum response expected from child:	Back-up questions:
	Usher brings candidate in.	Usher to examiner: **Hello, this is (child's name*).** Examiner: **Hello, *, my name's Jane/Ms Smith.**		
			Hello.	
		What's your surname?	*Silver*	**What's your family name?**
		How old are you, *?	*11*	**Are you 11?**
1	Shows candidate both **Find the Differences** pictures.	**Now, here are two pictures. My picture is nearly the same as yours, but some things are different.**		
	Points to the rucksack in each picture.	**For example, in my picture the rucksack's closed, but in your picture the rucksack's open. OK?**		
	Describes things without pointing.	**I'm going to say something about my picture. You tell me how your picture is different.**		1. Point at relevant difference/s. 2. Repeat statement. 3. Ask back-up question.
		In my picture, there are sausages on the fire.	*In my picture, there are eggs on the fire.*	**Are there sausages on the fire?**
		In my picture, the girl's wearing a blue T-shirt.	*In my picture, the girl's wearing a red T-shirt.*	**What colour is the girl's T-shirt?**
		In my picture, I can see two maps on the ground.	*In my picture, I can see one map.*	**How many maps can you see?**
		In my picture, the boy's sleeping.	*In my picture, the boy's reading.*	**What's the boy doing?**
		In my picture, the man's got a bottle on his belt.	*In my picture, the man's got a phone on his belt.*	**What has the man got on his belt?**
		In my picture, there's a flag. It's at the front of the tent.	*In my picture, the flag's at the back of the tent.*	**Is the flag at the front of the tent?**
2	Shows candidate both **favourite shop** information pages. Then points to candidate's information page.	**Ben and Jill like shopping. They both have a favourite shop. I don't know anything about Ben's favourite shop, but you do. So I'm going to ask you some questions.**		
	Points to the boy on candidate's information page. Asks the questions.	**Where is the shop?** **What is the name of the shop?** **Is the shop big or small?** **When does the shop open?** **What does Ben buy there?**	*(in) West Street* *Movies Now* *(it's) big* *(at) 9 o'clock* *DVDs*	Point at the information if necessary.
	Points to the girl on candidate's information page.	**Now you don't know anything about Jill's favourite shop, so you ask me some questions.**		

*Remember to use the child's name throughout the test.

Part	Examiner does this:	Examiner says this:	Minimum response expected from child:	Back-up questions:
	Responds using information on examiner's information page.	It's called First News.	*What's the name of the shop?*	Point at information cues if necessary.
		comics	*What does Jill buy there?*	
		It's in Forest Road.	*Where is the shop?*	
		at 7 o'clock	*When does the shop open?*	
		It's small.	*Is the shop big or small?*	
3	Shows candidate **Picture Story**. Allows time to look at the pictures.	These pictures tell a story. It's called 'The dog and the circus'. Just look at the pictures first.		
		Nick and Anna are going to the circus with their parents today. Their dog wants to go with them, but it must stay at home.		1. Point at the pictures. 2. Ask questions about the pictures.
		Now you tell the story.	*The family are driving to the circus.*	**Where are the family going?**
			The dog is jumping through the window.	**What's the dog doing now?**
			Now the dog's following the car.	**What's the dog doing now?**
			The family are watching the clowns but Nick and Anna are bored.	**What are the family doing?**
				Are Nick and Anna bored?
			The dog is playing with the clowns.	**What's the dog doing now?**
			Nick and Anna are laughing.	**Are Anna and Nick bored now?**
4	Puts the pictures away and turns to the candidate.	Now, let's talk about the things you do every day.		
		What time do you get up?	*(at) 7 o'clock*	**Do you get up at 7 o'clock?**
		How do you go to school?	*(by) bus*	**Do you go to school by bus?**
		What do you have for lunch?	*chicken*	**Do you have chicken for lunch?**
		Where do you play with your friends?	*(in the) playground*	**Do you play in the playground?**
		Tell me about your evening.	*I do my homework.*	**Do you do your homework?**
			I play computer games.	**Do you play computer games?**
			I watch TV.	**Do you watch TV?**
		OK, thank you, *.		
		Goodbye.	Goodbye.	

*Remember to use the child's name throughout the test.

Test 3 Answers

Listening

Part 1 (5 marks)
Lines should be drawn between:
1 Robert and the boy at the table, with a plate full of food
2 Harry and the man in blue jeans, dancing
3 Katy and the little girl dancing, with hair like a coconut
4 Sarah and the girl who's drinking
5 William and the man with a beard, looking at his watch

Part 2 (5 marks)
1 12/twelve   2 Tigers   3 Rockets   4 afternoon(s)
5 Boundary (correct spelling)

Part 3 (5 marks)
1 woman with red jacket and short dark hair – G – restaurant
2 man in uniform – H – station   3 woman in glasses – A – house
4 man with missing tooth – E – hospital
5 woman with gold handbag – C – hotel

Part 4 (5 marks)
1 A   2 B   3 C   4 A   5 C

Part 5 (5 marks)
1 Colour the sweater of the boy pushing the car – blue
2 Colour the skate on the ground – green
3 Write 'ROOM' under 'COMPUTER' on the sign
4 Draw and colour the mouth on the face of the teacher with the scarf – pink
5 Colour the empty bin – purple

TRANSCRIPT	*Hello. This is the Cambridge English Flyers Listening Test.*

Part 1   *Listen and look. There is one example.*

[pause]

WOMAN: Do you know the people at this party?
GIRL: Not everyone, but I know some of them. May, for example.
WOMAN: Which one is she?
GIRL: She's the little girl in the long yellow socks. She's just fallen over!

[pause]

Can you see the line? This is an example.

Now you listen and draw lines.

[pause]

1

WOMAN: Do you know that boy next to the table?
GIRL: Yes, that's my cousin, Robert.
WOMAN: Look at his plate – there's a lot of food on it!
GIRL: Yes. He always eats a lot at parties.

[pause]

2

WOMAN: Look at that man in the blue jeans. He's enjoying the party!
GIRL: That's my uncle Harry. He looks very funny when he's dancing.
WOMAN: I think he likes this music.
GIRL: Well, yes … he chose it!

[pause]

3

WOMAN: Who's that little girl over there – the one who's sleeping in the chair?

GIRL: Sorry, I don't know her. But I know the other little girl – the one who's dancing.
WOMAN: What's her name, then?
GIRL: Her name's Katy, but we call her 'Coconut'. Everyone likes her.

[pause]

4

GIRL: Can you see that girl who's holding a glass in her hand?
WOMAN: Yes – she's putting some ice into her drink.
GIRL: No, not her. I mean the girl who's drinking. Look!
WOMAN: Oh, yes. Sorry.
GIRL: That's my best friend, Sarah.
WOMAN: She looks nice, too. I want to meet her.

[pause]

5

WOMAN: I know that man with the beard, but I can't remember his name.
GIRL: Oh, that's William.
WOMAN: Why is he looking at his watch?
GIRL: It's seven o'clock – in a minute he's going to stop the music.
WOMAN: Why?
GIRL: So we can play games. It happens at all our parties!

[pause]

Now listen to Part 1 again.

[The recording is repeated.]

That is the end of Part 1.

[pause]

Part 2 *Listen and look. There is one example.*

[pause]

MAN: Hello. Can I help you?
BOY: Yes. I want to play football with the 'High Flyers' club.
MAN: I see. What's your name?
BOY: David. David Smith.
MAN: How do you spell that?
BOY: It's S-M-I-T-H.

[pause]

Can you see the answer? Now you listen and write.

[pause]

MAN: How old are you, David?
BOY: Is it important?
MAN: Yes. Children have to be eleven or older to play with the High Flyers.
BOY: Oh, that's OK. I'm twelve.
MAN: Good. Have you played football before?
BOY: Oh, yes. I played for my village team. They're called the Tigers. We played twice a week in the winter and the spring. I left the team because it's for younger children.

MAN: I understand. Well, that sounds fine. You'll be in our second team.
BOY: Oh – can't I be in your first team?
MAN: No, I'm sorry, David. Not until next year.
BOY: What's the second team called? Has it got a name?
MAN: Yes, it's called the 'Rockets'.
BOY: Mm. That's a good name! Does the team play on Saturday?
MAN: Yes, it does. In the afternoon. Is that a problem for you?
BOY: No, that's better for me because I have a guitar lesson in the morning.
MAN: OK. Now, the place, so listen carefully. We meet at Boundary Sports Centre …
BOY: Sorry, how do you spell that?
MAN: It's B-O-U-N-D-A-R-Y. The same name as the road.
BOY: All right.
MAN: Can your mum or dad bring you there?
BOY: Yes. My mum will bring me.
MAN: Excellent! Well, see you next month, David.
BOY: Thanks. Bye.

[pause]

Now listen to Part 2 again.

[The recording is repeated.]

That is the end of Part 2.

[pause]

Part 3 *Listen and look. There is one example.*

[pause]

Mr Brown is a taxi driver. A policewoman is asking him questions. Who did Mr Brown take to these places?

[pause]

WOMAN: Now, Mr Brown, you drove a lot of people in your taxi yesterday. I want you to tell me about them. What did they look like? Where did you take them?
MAN: Well, the first person was a man with short grey hair and a grey moustache. I think he was a teacher because he had a bag of books. I took him to the school on Forest Road. That was in the morning.

[pause]

Can you see the letter B? Now you listen and write a letter in each box.

[pause]

WOMAN: Who else did you take?
MAN: Erm, there was a woman with short dark hair … she had a red jacket on. She was outside the City Bank and she waved at me. She wanted a taxi because it was raining. I took her to a restaurant – you know, that expensive place on Park Street.

[pause]

WOMAN: Can you remember any other people?

MAN: Oh, yes. For example, there was a man in a uniform. I remember him well because he didn't speak and he looked angry. I took him to the station.

[pause]

WOMAN: Go on.

MAN: In the afternoon, I took a young woman to a house. It was in West Street. I can't remember her face very well, but I can remember her glasses. Yours are round but hers were square. They looked funny, I thought.

[pause]

WOMAN: Did you take anyone else in the afternoon?

MAN: Yes. I was driving back to the city centre when I saw a man with his hand out. He told me to take him to the hospital. When he smiled he looked strange, because one of his teeth was missing.

[pause]

WOMAN: That's interesting. Anyone else?

MAN: Yes, in the evening I met a man and a woman at the airport. The man had a large suitcase. He didn't get in my taxi. He got on a bus. But I took the woman to a hotel. I remember her handbag because it was gold … the colour, I mean. It looked nice. I'd like to speak to her again soon.

WOMAN: Oh, yes. Why?

MAN: Because she left it in my taxi!

[pause]

Now listen to Part 3 again.

[The recording is repeated.]

That is the end of Part 3.

[pause]

Part 4 *Listen and look. There is one example.*

[pause]

What's Emma going to do?

[pause]

GIRL: What shall I do, Grandma? I'm bored.

WOMAN: Why don't you draw a picture for me?

GIRL: No. I did that this morning. Can we make a cake together?

WOMAN: Not now, Emma. I have to make lunch soon. Here – look at these old photos.

GIRL: All right. I'll do that.

[pause]

Can you see the tick? Now you listen and tick the box.

[pause]

1 Which dog is in the photo?

GIRL: Grandma, whose dog is it in this photo?

WOMAN: I can't come now, dear. What does it look like?

GIRL: It's a white dog with black spots.

WOMAN: Has it got long hair?

GIRL: No, it hasn't. But it's got a very short tail.

WOMAN: Ah, that's Pepper. He was my dog when I was a little girl.

[pause]

2 Which picture shows Grandma when she was a child?

GIRL: Oh, look. Here's a picture of you on the beach, in a funny hat.

WOMAN: Let me see. Oh, yes! It was very hot that summer! We all had to wear hats. Look at my dress. It's so dirty!

GIRL: Who's the girl with the towel over her shoulders?

WOMAN: That's my friend, Sally. And the taller girl in shorts is her sister.

[pause]

3 What was Grandpa's job?

GIRL: I want to be a photographer when I'm a grown-up.

WOMAN: Like your grandfather.

GIRL: But Grandpa was a mechanic – you told me!

WOMAN: That was his job, but his hobby was taking pictures …

GIRL: And singing?

WOMAN: Mm, but only when he was a young man.

[pause]

4 What are Emma's sweets made from?

GIRL: Try one of these sweets, Grandma.

WOMAN: Thank you. Mm! This tastes nice. Is it apple?

GIRL: I think it tastes like pear.

WOMAN: Well, what is it made from? Tell me.

GIRL: It says here: 'Made from watermelons.'

WOMAN: Oh!

[pause]

5 What's Emma going to have for lunch?

GIRL: What's for lunch today, Grandma? Are we going to have pasta?

WOMAN: Sorry, Emma, I haven't got any. What about a nice chicken sandwich?

GIRL: Yes please, Grandma, but without salad. I hate it!

WOMAN: All right, dear. I'll make it for you now.

[pause]

Now listen to Part 4 again.

[The recording is repeated.]

That is the end of Part 4.

[pause]

Part 5 Listen and look at the picture. There is one example.

[pause]

MAN: Would you like to colour this picture of a school playground?
GIRL: Yes, please. Can I colour one of the girls?
MAN: All right. Can you see the girl who's hopping?
GIRL: Yes. She looks happy!
MAN: Well, colour her skirt brown.

[pause]

Can you see the girl's brown skirt? This is an example.

Now you listen and colour and write and draw.

[pause]

1

MAN: Can you colour one of the boys, please?
GIRL: The one who's pushing the little car?
MAN: Yes, OK. But only his sweater.
GIRL: Shall I do it blue? That's a nice colour.
MAN: Yes, that's fine.

[pause]

2

MAN: Now, I'd like you to colour something else. There are two skates in the picture. Can you see them?
GIRL: Yes, shall I colour the one on the wall?
MAN: No, the other one. It's on the ground. This time use green.
GIRL: OK. I'm colouring it now.

[pause]

3

GIRL: What can I colour next?
MAN: Don't colour anything. I'd like you to write a word.
GIRL: OK. What shall I write?
MAN: Can you see the word 'COMPUTER'? It's on the left of the picture. Under it please write the word 'ROOM'.
GIRL: OK. I can do that.

[pause]

4

MAN: Can you draw and colour something now, please?
GIRL: Yes, of course. I like drawing. What shall I draw?
MAN: Look at the teacher ...
GIRL: Which one? The one who's wearing a scarf?
MAN: Yes, that's right. Draw a mouth on her face, and then colour it pink.

[pause]

5

GIRL: What shall I colour now?
MAN: Well, there are two bins in the playground.
GIRL: Yes, can I colour the one that's full?
MAN: No, colour the empty one. It's easier. What colour do you want to use?
GIRL: Er, purple.
MAN: Well done. That looks excellent.

[pause]

Now listen to Part 5 again.

[The recording is repeated.]

That is the end of the Flyers Listening Test.

Reading and Writing

Part 1 (10 marks)

1 an umbrella   2 meals   3 stations
4 paper   5 universities   6 silver   7 cheese
8 plastic   9 a tent   10 offices

Part 2 (7 marks)

1 yes   2 no   3 yes   4 no   5 no
6 yes   7 no

Part 3 (5 marks)

1 B   2 G   3 E   4 A   5 C

Part 4 (6 marks)

1 early   2 hours   3 hard   4 smell
5 torch   6 Socks finds Harry

Part 5 (7 marks)

1 aunt
2 (different) people (in the street)
3 (the/some) treasure
4 (big) rucksack/backpack
5 the/a (number 14) bus
6 policeman
7 the (town's) newspaper

Part 6 (10 marks)

1 until   2 enough   3 carry   4 every
5 which   6 quickly   7 if   8 it   9 have
10 only

Part 7 (5 marks)

1 than   2 There   3 like/love   4 ask/tell
5 to

Speaking

Part	Examiner does this:	Examiner says this:	Minimum response expected from child:	Back-up questions:
	Usher brings candidate in.	Usher to examiner: **Hello, this is (child's name*).**		
		Examiner: **Hello, *. My name's Jane/Ms Smith.**		
		What's your surname?	Hello.	**What's your family name?**
		How old are you, *?	*Silver* *11*	**Are you 11?**
1	Shows candidate both **Find the Differences** pictures.	**Now, here are two pictures. My picture is nearly the same as yours, but some things are different.**		
	Points to the door in each picture.	**For example, in my picture the door of the house is open, but in your picture it's closed. OK?**		
		I'm going to say something about my picture. You tell me how your picture is different.		1. Point at relevant difference/s. 2. Repeat statement. 3. Ask back-up question.
	Describes things without pointing.	**In my picture, the duck is brown and yellow.**	*In my picture, it's purple and green.*	**What colour is the duck?**
		In my picture, there are three people. Only one person has got a rucksack.	*In my picture, three people have got rucksacks.*	**How many people have got rucksacks?**
		In my picture, the man is carrying an umbrella.	*In my picture, he isn't carrying an umbrella.*	**Is the man carrying an umbrella?**
		In my picture, I can see a frog on the small rock.	*In my picture, I can see a frog on the big rock.*	**Is the frog on a small rock?**
		In my picture, the boy in the boat is holding a map.	*In my picture, he's holding a flag.*	**What's the boy holding?**
		In my picture, there's a monkey. It's on a swing.	*In my picture, the monkey is in the tree.*	**Is the monkey on the swing?**
2	Shows candidate both **bus** information pages. Then points to candidate's information page.	**David and Helen both go to school by bus. I don't know anything about David's bus, but you do. So I'm going to ask you some questions.**		
	Points to the boy on candidate's information page.	**What number is David's bus?**	*(It's bus number) 12.*	Point at the information if necessary.
		What time does David's bus leave?	*(at) twenty past eight*	
	Asks the questions.	**What colour is it?**	*green*	
		Where does David get on his bus?	*(outside the) library*	
		What's the name of the bus driver?	*Mr Plane*	
	Points to the girl on candidate's information page.	**Now you don't know anything about Helen's bus, so you ask me some questions.**		

*Remember to use the child's name throughout the test.

Part	Examiner does this:	Examiner says this:	Minimum response expected from child:	Back-up questions:
	Responds using information on examiner's information page.	outside her house	**Where does Helen get on her bus?**	Point at information cues if necessary.
		at ten to eight	**What time does Helen's bus leave?**	
		It's blue.	**What colour is Helen's bus?**	
		It's bus number 8.	**What number is Helen's bus?**	
		Mrs Race	**What's the name of the bus driver?**	
3	Shows candidate **Picture Story**. Allows time to look at the pictures.	**These pictures tell a story. It's called 'Sarah's new sledge'. Just look at the pictures first.**		
		Sarah wants to play in the snow with her friend, but her grandmother is saying, 'First you must help me to do the shopping. I can't carry everything.'		1. Point at the pictures. 2. Ask questions about the pictures.
		Now you tell the story.	*Sarah and her grandmother have a lot of bags.*	*Have they got a lot of bags?*
			Sarah's looking at the sledge.	*What's Sarah looking at?*
			Sarah and her grandmother are buying the sledge.	*What are Sarah and her grandmother doing? What are they buying?*
			All the shopping bags are on the sledge. Sarah's pulling the sledge.	*What's on the sledge?*
			Sarah and her friend are playing with the new sledge in the snow. They're having fun.	*What's Sarah doing?* *Is she having fun?*
4	Puts the pictures away and turns to the candidate.	**Now let's talk about birthdays.**		
		When's your birthday?	*(It's in) July*	**Is your birthday in July?**
		How old will you be on your next birthday?	*thirteen*	**Will you be thirteen?**
		What do you like eating on your birthday?	*cake*	**Do you like eating cake?**
		What present would you like?	*a bicycle*	**Would you like a bicycle?**
		Tell me about your last birthday.	*My parents gave me a computer.* *I had a party.* *It was fun.*	**What did your parents give you?** **Did you have a party?** **Was it fun?**
		OK, thank you, *. **Goodbye.**	**Goodbye.**	

*Remember to use the child's name throughout the test.

COMBINED STARTERS, MOVERS AND FLYERS THEMATIC VOCABULARY LIST

For ease of reference, vocabulary is arranged in semantic groups or themes. Some words appear under more than one heading.

In addition to the topics, notions and concepts listed for the syllabus, the following categories appear:

- useful words and expressions
- adjectives
- determiners
- adverbs
- prepositions
- conjunctions
- pronouns
- verbs
- modals
- question words
- names

s – first appears at *Starters*
m – first appears at *Movers*
f – first appears at *Flyers*

ANIMALS

- *s* animal
- *m* bat
- *m* bear
- *s* bird
- *f* butterfly
- *m* cage
- *f* camel
- *s* cat
- *s* chicken
- *s* cow
- *s* crocodile
- *f* dinosaur
- *s* dog
- *m* dolphin
- *s* duck
- *s* elephant
- *s* fish (s & pl)
- *m* fly
- *s* frog
- *f* fur
- *s* giraffe
- *s* goat
- *s* hippo
- *s* horse
- *f* insect
- *m* kangaroo
- *m* kitten
- *m* lion
- *s* lizard
- *s* monkey
- *s* mouse/mice
- *f* octopus
- *m* panda
- *m* parrot
- *m* pet
- *m* puppy
- *m* rabbit
- *m* shark
- *s* sheep (s & pl)
- *s* snake
- *s* spider
- *f* swan
- *s* tail
- *s* tiger
- *m* whale
- *f* wing
- *s* zoo

THE BODY & FACE

- *s* arm
- *m* back
- *m* beard
- *m* blond(e)
- *s* body
- *m* curly
- *s* ear
- *s* eye
- *s* face
- *m* fair
- *s* foot/feet
- *s* hair
- *s* hand
- *s* head
- *s* leg
- *m* moustache
- *s* mouth
- *m* neck
- *s* nose
- *m* shoulder
- *s* smile
- *m* stomach
- *m* straight
- *m* tooth/teeth

CLOTHES

- *s* bag
- *f* belt
- *s* clothes
- *m* coat
- *s* dress
- *s* glasses
- *f* glove
- *s* handbag
- *s* hat
- *s* jacket
- *s* jeans
- *f* pocket
- *f* ring
- *m* scarf
- *s* shirt
- *s* shoe
- *f* shorts
- *s* skirt
- *s* sock
- *f* spot
- *f* spotted
- *f* stripe
- *f* striped
- *m* sweater
- *f* tights
- *s* trousers
- *s* T-shirt
- *f* umbrella
- *f* uniform
- *s* watch
- *s* wear

COLOURS

- *s* black
- *s* blue
- *s* brown
- *f* gold
- *s* green
- *s* grey (or gray)
- *s* orange
- *s* pink
- *s* purple
- *s* red
- *f* silver
- *s* white
- *s* yellow

FAMILY & FRIENDS

m aunt
s baby
s boy
s brother
s child/children
s cousin
s dad(dy)
m daughter
s family
s father
s friend
s girl
m granddaughter
s grandfather
s grandma
s grandmother
s grandpa
m grandparent
m grandson
m grown up
f husband
s live
s man/men
f married
s Miss
s mother
s Mr
s Mrs
s mum(my)
s old
m parent
s person/people
s sister
m son
f surname
s their
s them
s they
m uncle
s us
s we
f wife
s woman/women
s you
s young
s your

FOOD & DRINK

s apple
s banana
s bean
f biscuit (US cookie)
m bottle
m bowl
s bread
s breakfast
s burger
f butter
s cake
f candy (UK sweets)
s carrot
m cheese

s chicken
s chips (US fries)
f chocolate
f chopsticks
s coconut
m coffee
f cookie (UK biscuit)
m cup
s dinner
s drink (n & v)
s eat
s egg
s fish
f flour
s food
f fork
s fries (UK chips)
s fruit
m glass of
s grape
m hungry
s ice cream
f jam
s juice
f knife
s lemon
s lemonade
s lime
s lunch
s mango
f meal
s meat
s milk
s onion
s orange
m pasta
s pea
s pear
f pepper
m picnic
f piece
s pineapple
f pizza
f plate
s potato
s rice
m salad
f salt
m sandwich
s sausage
f smell
f snack
m soup
f spoon
f sugar
s supper
f sweets (US candy)
f taste
m tea
m thirsty
s tomato
m vegetable
s water
s watermelon

HEALTH

f chemist('s)
m cold
m cough
f dentist
m doctor
m earache
m fine
m headache
m hospital
m hurt
f ill
m matter (What's the matter?)
f medicine
m nurse
f problem
m stomach-ache
m temperature
m toothache

THE HOME

m address
s apartment
s armchair
m balcony
m basement
s bath
s bathroom
s bed
s bedroom
m blanket
s bookcase
s box
f brush
s camera
s chair
s clock
f comb
s computer
f cooker
s cupboard
s desk
f diary
s dining room
s doll
s door
m downstairs
m dream
m elevator
f envelope
m fan
s flat
s floor
s flower
f fridge
s garden
s hall
m home
s house
f key
s kitchen
s lamp
f letter

m lift
s living room
s mat
s mirror
f money
s painting
s phone
s picture
s radio
s room
f secret
f shelf
m shopping
m shower
s sleep
f soap
s sofa
m stairs
f stamp
f swing
s table
f telephone
s television/TV
f toilet
m toothbrush
m towel
s toy
s tree
m upstairs
s wall
m wash (n)
s watch
s window

MATERIALS

f card
f glass
f gold
f metal
f paper
f plastic
f silver
f wood
f wool

NUMBERS

s Cardinals: 1–20
m Cardinals: 21–100
f Cardinals: 101–1000
m Ordinals: 1st–20th
f Ordinals: 21st–31st

PLACES & DIRECTIONS

m above
f airport
m bank
s behind
s between
f bookshop
f bridge
m bus station

f bus stop
m café
f castle
f chemist('s)
m cinema
f circus
f club
f college
f corner
f east
f end
f factory
m farm
f fire station
f front
f get to
s here
m hospital
f hotel
s in
s in front of
f kilometre(s) (US) kilometer(s)
f left
m library
f London
m map
m market
f museum
s next to
f north
s on
f over
s park
m place
s playground
f police station
f post office
f restaurant
f right
m road
s shop (US store)
f south
m square
f station
s store (UK shop)
m straight
f straight on
s street
m supermarket
m swimming pool
f theatre
s there
s under
f university
f way
f west
s zoo

SCHOOL

s alphabet
s answer
f art

s ask
f bin
s board
s book
s bookcase
s class
s classroom
s close
f club
f college
s colour
f competition
s computer
s correct
s cross
s cupboard
s desk
f dictionary
s door
s draw(ing)
s English
s eraser
f exam (examination)
s example
s find
f flag
s floor
f geography
f glue
f group
f history
m homework
s know
f language
s learn
s lesson
s letter (as in alphabet)
s line
s listen (to)
s look
f maths
m mistake
s name
s number
s open
s page
s part
s pen
s pencil
s picture
s playground
s question
s read
s right (as in correct)
s rubber
f rucksack
s ruler
s school
f science
f scissors
s sentence
f shelf
s spell

s stand (up)
s story
f student
f subject
s teacher
s tell
s test (n & v)
m text
s tick (n & v)
s understand
f university
s wall
s window
s word
s write
f zero

SPORTS & LEISURE

s badminton
s ball
s baseball
s basketball
m bat
s beach
s bike
s boat
s book
s bounce
s camera
s catch
m CD
m comic/comic book
f conversation
f diary
s doll
s draw(ing)
s drive
f drum
m DVD
s enjoy
s favourite
m film
s fish(ing)
f flashlight
s fly
s football (US soccer)
s game
f golf
s guitar
s hit
s hobby
s hockey
m holiday
f hotel
s jump
s kick (n & v)
s kite
s listen (to)
f magazine
m movie
m music
s paint(ing)

m party
s photo
s piano
s picture
s play (with)
f player (as in CD player)
f postcard
m present
f programme (US program)
f pyramid
f race
s radio
s read
s ride (n & v)
f rucksack
s run
m sail
f score
s sing
m skate
f ski
f sledge
f snowball
f snowman
s soccer (UK football)
s song
s sport
m sports centre
s story
f suitcase
m swim (n)
m swimming pool
f swing
s table tennis
f tape recorder
f team
s television/TV
s tennis
f tent
s throw
f torch
m towel
s toy
s TV/television
f umbrella
m video
f volleyball
m walk (n)
s watch

TIME

f a.m.
m after
s afternoon
m age
f ago
m always
f autumn
m before
s birthday
f century
f Christmas

s clock
f date
s day
f early
s end
s evening
m every
f future
f half
f hour
f late
f later
f midday
f midnight
f minute
f month
s morning
m never
s night
f o'clock
f p.m.
f past
f quarter
m sometimes
f spring
f summer
f time
s today
f tomorrow
f tonight
s watch
m week
m weekend
f winter
f year
m yesterday

The days of the week:
m Sunday
m Monday
m Tuesday
m Wednesday
m Thursday
m Friday
m Saturday

The months of the year:
f January
f February
f March
f April
f May
f June
f July
f August
f September
f October
f November
f December

TOYS

s ball
s baseball
s basketball

s bike
s car
s doll
s football
s game
s helicopter
s kite
s lorry (US truck)
s monster
s plane
s robot
s toy
s train
m treasure
s truck (UK lorry)

TRANSPORT

f airport
f ambulance
f bicycle
s bike
s boat
s bus
m bus station
s car
m drive (n)
s drive (v)
m driver
f fire engine
s fly
s go
s helicopter
s lorry (US truck)
s motorbike
s plane
m ride (n)
s ride (v)
f rocket
s run
f station
s swim
f taxi
m ticket
f traffic
s train
s truck (UK lorry)
s walk

WEATHER

m cloud
m cloudy
f fog
f foggy
f ice
m rain
m rainbow
f sky
m snow
f storm
s sun

m sunny
m weather
m wind
m windy

WORK

f actor/actress
f airport
f ambulance
f artist
f astronaut
f business
f businessman/woman
f circus
m clown
f cook
f dentist
m doctor
f engineer
f factory
m farmer
f fireman/woman
f footballer
m hospital
f job
f journalist
f mechanic
f meeting
f news
f newspaper
m nurse
f office
f painter
f photographer
f pilot
m pirate
f police station
f policeman/woman
f queen
f secretary
f singer
s teacher
f tennis player
f waiter
m work

THE WORLD AROUND US

f air
s beach
f bridge
f castle
f cave
m city
m country(side)
f desert
f environment
m field
f fire
m forest
f future

m grass
m ground
f hill
m island
m jungle
m lake
m leaf/leaves
m moon
m mountain
f planet
m plant
f pyramid
m river
m road
m rock
s sand
s sea
s shell
f sky
f space
m star
s street
s sun
m town
s tree
m village
s water
m waterfall
f wood
m world

USEFUL WORDS & EXPRESSIONS

s bye (-bye)
m come on!
f excellent
m excuse me
s goodbye
s hello
s I don't know
s no
s oh
s oh dear
s OK
s pardon
s please
s right
m see you!
s so
s sorry
s thank you
s thanks
s then
s well
s well done
s wow
s yes

ADJECTIVES

m afraid
m all
m all right
s angry
m awake
m back
m bad
s beautiful
m best
m better
s big
f bored
m boring
m bottom
f brave
f broken
m busy
m careful
f cheap
s clean
m clever
s closed
m cloudy
m cold
s correct
f dangerous
f dark
f dear
m different
m difficult
s dirty
s double
f dry
f each
f early
m easy
f empty
s English
f enough
m every
f excellent
f excited
m exciting
f expensive
f extinct
m famous
f far
f fast
m fat
s favourite
m fine
m first
f friendly
f front
f full
f fun
s funny
f glass
f gold
s good
s great

f half
s happy
f hard
f heavy
s her
f high
s his
f horrible
m hot
m hungry
f ill
f important
f interesting
s its
f kind
m last
f late
f left (as in direction)
f light
f little
s long
m loud
f lovely
f low
f many
f married
f metal
f missing
m more
m most
s my
m naughty
s new
f next
s nice
f noisy
s old
s open
f other
s our
f paper
f plastic
f poor
m quick
m quiet
f ready
f rich
s right (correct)
f right (as in direction)
m round
s sad
f same
m second
s short
f silver
f single
m slow
s small
f soft
s sorry
f spotted
m square
m straight

f strange
f striped
m strong
f sure
m surprised
m tall
m terrible
s their
m thin
m third
m thirsty
f tidy
m tired
m top
s ugly
f unfriendly
f unhappy
f untidy
f warm
m weak
m well
m wet
m windy
m worse
m worst
m wrong
s young
s your

DETERMINERS

s a/an
f a few
f a little
s a lot of
m all
m another
m any
m both
f each
m every
s lots of
s many
m more
m most
f much
s my
s no
s one
f other
s some
s that
s the
s these
s this
s those

ADVERBS

s a lot
f after
s again
f ago
m all right

f already
f also
m always
f anywhere
f away
m back
m badly
f before
m best
m better
m carefully
m down
m downstairs
f early
f else
f ever
f everywhere
f far
f fast
m first
f hard
s here
m how
m how much
m how often
m inside
f just
m last
f late
f later
s lots
m loudly
m more
m most
f much
m near
m never
f next
s not
s now
f nowhere
f of course (not)
m off
m often
m on
f once
m only
m out
m outside
f over
f perhaps
m quickly
m quietly
m slowly
f so
m sometimes
f somewhere
f soon
f still
f straight on
f suddenly
s then

s there
s today
f together
f tomorrow
f tonight
s too
f twice
m up
m upstairs
f usually
s very
m well
m when
m worse
m worst
m yesterday
f yet

PREPOSITIONS

s about
m above
f across
m after
s at
m before
s behind
m below
s between
m by
m down
f during
f far
s for
f for (prep of time)
f from
m in (prep of time)
s in front of
m inside
f into
s like
m near
s next to
s of
m off
s on
m on (prep of time)
m opposite
m out of
m outside
f over
f past
m round
f since
m than
f through
s to
s under
f until
s with
f without

CONJUNCTIONS

f after
s and
m because
f before
s but
f if
s or
f so
m than
m when

PRONOUNS

m all
m another
f anyone
f anything
m both
f each
f else
f enough
f everyone
f everything
s he
s her
s hers
s him
s his
s I
s it
s its
s me
s mine
m more
m most
f much
f no-one
m nothing
s one
f other
s ours
s she
f someone
m something
s that
s theirs
s them
s these
s they
s this
s those
s us
s we
f where
m which
m who
s you
s yours

VERBS

Irregular:

s be
f begin
f break
m bring
f burn
m buy
s catch (a ball)
m catch (a bus)
s choose
s come
f cut
s do
s draw
s drink
s drive
s eat
f fall
f fall over
f feel (like)
s find
f find out
s fly
f forget
s get
f get (off/on/to)
m get (un)dressed
m get up
s give
s go
f go out
m go shopping
f grow
s have
s have (got)
m have (got) to
f hear
m hide
s hit
s hold
m hurt
s know
s learn
f leave
s let
f let's
f lie (down)
m lose
s make
m mean
f meet
m must
s put
m put on
s read
s ride
s run
s say
s see
f sell
f send

s sing
s sit (down)
s sleep
f smell (v intr)
f smell (like) (v tr)
f speak
s spell
f spend
s stand (up)
f steal
s swim
f swing
m take
m take (a bus)
m take (a photo)
m take off
f take time
f teach
s tell
m think
s throw
s understand
m wake up
s wear
f will
f win
f won't
s write

Regular:

s add
f agree
s answer
f arrive
s ask
f ask for
f believe
s bounce
f brush
f burn
m call
f camp
m carry
s clean
m climb
s close
s colour
f comb
s complete
m cook
s cross
m cry
m dance
f decide
m dream
m drop
m email
f end
s enjoy
f explain
f fetch
m film
f finish

m fish
f follow
f glue
f guess
f happen
f hate
m help
m hop
m invite
s jump
s kick
m laugh
s learn
s like
s listen (to)
s live
s look
f look after
s look at
m look for
f look (like)
s love
f mind
f mix
m move
m need
s open
s paint
s phone
s pick up
m plant
s play (with)
s point
s point to
f post
f prefer
f pull
f push
f race
m rain
f remember
m sail
f score
m shop
m shout
s show
m skate
f ski
m skip
f sledge
s smile
m snow
f sound (like)
s start
f stay
s stop
f study
s talk
f taste (like)
s test
m text
f thank
s tick

f tidy
s try
f turn
f turn (off/on)
f use
m video
f visit
m wait
s walk
s want
m wash
s watch
s wave
f whisper
f whistle
f wish
m work

MODALS

s can/cannot/can't
m could
f may
f might
m must
m shall
f should
m would

QUESTION WORDS

s how
s how many
m how much
s how old
s what
m when
s where
s which
s who
s whose
m why

NAMES

s Alex
s Ann
s Anna
s Ben
f Betty
s Bill
m Charlie
m Daisy
s Dan
f David
f Emma
m Fred
f George
s Grace
f Harry
f Helen
f Holly
m Jack
m Jane
s Jill
m Jim
m John
f Katy
s Kim
m Lily
s Lucy
m Mary
s May
f Michael
s Nick
s Pat
m Paul
m Peter
f Richard
f Robert
m Sally
s Sam
f Sarah
s Sue
s Tom
s Tony
m Vicky
f William